HOCKEY

BY MARTY GITLIN

CONTENT CONSULTANT
KAREN THATCHER
US OLYMPIC HOCKEY PLAYER

Published by ABDO Publishing Company, PO Box 398166, Minneapolis, MN 55439. Copyright © 2012 by Abdo Consulting Group, Inc. International copyrights reserved in all countries. No part of this book may be reproduced in any form without written permission from the publisher. SportsZone™ is a trademark and logo of ABDO Publishing Company.

Printed in the United States of America,
North Mankato, Minnesota
102011
012012

Editor: Chrös McDougall
Copy Editor: Anna Comstock
Series Design and Cover Production: Craig Hinton
Interior Production: Kelsey Oseid

Photo Credits: Gene J. Puskar/AP Images, cover (bottom), 45; Alexei Toiskin/iStockphoto, cover (top); Michael Caulfield/AP Images, 1; Robert Riger/Getty Images, 5, 35; Focus on Sport/Getty Images, 9; AP Images, 10, 15, 27, 31, 58 (middle); Ancient Art & Architecture Collection Ltd/Alamy, 17; Steve White/AP Images, 23, 58 (top); Rob Engelhardt/Erie Times-News/AP Images, 24; Alvin Quinn/AP Images, 29; Les/AP Images, 32; Bruce Bennett/Getty Images, 20, 38, 43, 58 (bottom); Steve Babineau/NHLI via Getty Images, 41, 59 (top); Kevork Djansezian/AP Images, 48, 59 (middle); Frank Gunn/AP Images, 52; Nam Y. Huh/AP Images, 55, 59 (bottom); Paul Sancya/AP Images, 56

Library of Congress Cataloging-in-Publication Data
Gitlin, Marty
  Hockey / by Marty Gitlin.
     p. cm. -- (Best sport ever)
  Includes index.
  ISBN 978-1-61783-144-7
  1. Hockey--Juvenile literature. I. Title.
  GV847.25.G585 2012
  796.962--dc23
                          2011034111

TABLE OF CONTENTS

"DO YOU BELIEVE IN MIRACLES?"

F ew Americans were thinking about ice hockey during the winter of 1980. There were too many disturbing developments at home and around the world occupying their minds.

A fanatical group of college students in Iran had taken 52 hostages from the US embassy. Americans fretted over whether any of them would come home alive. Meanwhile, tensions grew between the Soviet Union and the United States. The Soviet Union had invaded Afghanistan. That upset the US government.

At the time, the Olympic Winter Games and Summer Games were held in the same year. Today they are held two years apart. The United States was considering a boycott of the 1980 summer

The 1980 US Olympic hockey team celebrates after scoring against the heavily favored Soviet Union team in Lake Placid, New York.

Games, which were to be held in the Soviet Union. And indeed, the huge US team did not participate.

Back at home, the US economy was struggling. Prices for everyday items were skyrocketing. Unemployment was high. And millions of Americans worried about how they were going to pay their bills.

So even when the Olympic Winter Games started that February in Lake Placid, New York, few people were thinking about hockey. After all, on top of the hard times, the US team appeared to have little chance of winning a gold medal.

The Soviet Team

The Soviet Union's national hockey team at the time was considered one of the best teams ever—in any sport. And it was coming into the 1980 Games as the four-time defending Olympic champion.

NHL WELCOMED

Canada and the United States have gained great success in Olympic competition in recent years. The primary reason is that the NHL began allowing its players to compete. The International Olympic Committee opened up the Games to professional athletes in the late 1980s. But since the Winter Games are held during the NHL season, the league still did not permit its players to compete. That changed in 1998. The league decided to halt play so its athletes could participate in the Olympics. That resulted in both Canada and the United States playing for the gold medal in both the 2002 and 2010 Olympic Winter Games.

The Soviet team was made up of the best players that country had to offer. The US team, on the other hand, was filled with young and relatively unknown players. Professional players were not allowed to compete in the Olympics at that time. That meant the top US players—those who were playing in the National Hockey League (NHL)—could not play. Instead, the US team could only use amateurs, who are players that are not paid to compete. So Team USA was made up of the top college hockey players from around the country.

Most believed Team USA would be no match for the talented Soviets. After all, the Soviets had crushed a team of NHL All-Stars 6–0 in a game the previous year. They then showed their might against the 1980 US Olympic team three days before the start of the Winter Games. The two teams played an exhibition game. The Soviet Union dominated Team USA, winning 10–3.

Even so, Team USA got off to a strong start in the Games. It opened Olympic play by tying a strong Sweden team 2–2. The US team followed up that game with dominant victories over Czechoslovakia, Norway, Romania, and West Germany. The team averaged an impressive five goals per game during the first round. Along with Finland, Sweden, and the Soviet Union, Team USA qualified for the final round.

The final round had a unique format. The United States and Sweden had qualified from the Blue Division. Finland and the Soviet Union had qualified from the Red Division. Each team would play two more games, one against each team from the other division. Meanwhile, the first-round result against the inner-division opponent would carry over to the final round. A win was worth two points and a tie was worth one. At the end, the team with the most points would win.

Team USA had already tied Sweden in the first round to earn one point. In the final round, the team would have to face the Soviet Union and Finland. Despite the United States' successes in the first round, most people still believed it would be no match for the Soviets. After all, the Soviet Union had won 21 straight Olympic hockey games going into its contest against Team USA.

A Miracle Unfolding

The puck dropped to the ice to start the much-anticipated game between Team USA and the Soviet Union.

Something strange soon began to happen. The Soviets were showing that they had more talent. But the gritty US players battled hard and stayed in the game. The Soviets unleashed 18 shots toward US goaltender Jim Craig during the first period

Soviet right winger Aleksandr Maltsev scores on US goalie Jim Craig during the second period in the 1980 Olympics. The goal gave the Soviets a 3–2 lead.

Team USA's victory over the Soviet Union has come to be known as the Miracle on Ice. Many consider it to be the greatest upset in sports history.

alone. Meanwhile, Team USA managed just eight shots on goal. Yet when the buzzer sounded ending the period, the score was tied at 2–2.

The Soviets surprised many by benching legendary goalie Vladislav Tretiak after the first period. It was a controversial decision. Many considered him to be the best goalie in the world at the time. Tretiak's absence gave the US players more hope for a win.

Few US fans were able to watch the game live. However, the game's result was not widely known when they watched on tape delay. As the US players continued to play well, fans around the country became more intrigued. To many of them, this was more than a simple hockey game. The United States and the Soviet Union had experienced tense relations since World War II ended in 1945. The countries were considered the world's two superpowers, and they did not always agree.

The US players were gaining confidence. They were not gaining on the scoreboard, though. The Soviets led 3–2 with 12 minutes left in the game. But soon, US center Mark Johnson received a pass from right wing Dave Silk. Johnson then slid the puck past Soviet goaltender Vladimir Myshkin. The score was tied 3–3. And just a little more than one minute later, US left wing Mike Eruzione fired another shot into the back of net.

The United States suddenly led 4–3. The home crowd waved a sea of American flags. Their team held on for dear life. And as the final seconds ticked off the clock, television broadcaster Al Michaels made perhaps the most famous call in sports television history.

"Do you believe in miracles?" he shouted. "Yes!"

IT'S ALL IN THE WRIST

The game-winning goal by Mike Eruzione against the Soviet Union in the 1980 Olympic Winter Games was off a wrist shot. To execute a wrist shot, a player holds the stick with the top hand down and close to the body. The player then brings the puck back closer to his or her back foot. Then the player cups the puck and controls it near the heel of the stick blade. As the player transfers his or her weight from the back foot to the front foot, he or she sweeps the puck toward the goal with force.

The Soviet players stood stunned. The US players went crazy on the ice. *Sports Illustrated* writer E. M. Swift described the celebration:

> It was bizarre. It was beautiful. Upflung sticks slowly cartwheeled into the rafters. The American players—in pairs rather than in one great glop—hugged and danced and rolled on one another. In the streets of Lake Placid and across the country, it was more of the same. A spontaneous rally choked the streets outside the Olympic Ice Center, snarling bus traffic.

Going for the Gold

The US victory became known as the Miracle on Ice. But Team USA still had work to do in order to secure the gold medal. The United States faced Finland two days later. The Soviet Union faced

Sweden. To secure the gold medal, Team USA would need to win.

For the sixth time in seven games, the United States fell behind 1–0. Team USA traded goals with the rugged Finns to make the score 2–1. Then the US squad scored three goals in a 14-minute flurry in the third period. And once again, Johnson played hero. He assisted on the go-ahead goal and scored the final goal. The United States had a 4–2 victory and its first hockey gold medal in 20 years.

Nobody overlooked Craig, who saved shot after shot in each game. But he refused to take the credit. Instead, he thanked his teammates for helping him keep the puck out of the net.

AFTER "THE MIRACLE"

Life went on without professional hockey for most of the amateur US players who helped win the 1980 Olympic gold medal. But for coach Herb Brooks and several of the most talented players on the team, the NHL was calling. Brooks coached four NHL teams during a seven-year period. He earned five playoff berths. He also guided the US team to a silver medal in the 2002 Games. Tragedy struck a year later, though, when he was killed in a car accident.

Several US players went on to star in the NHL. Defenseman Mike Ramsey was a four-time All-Star in 18 seasons. Fellow defensemen Ken Morrow helped the New York Islanders win four straight Stanley Cup titles during the early 1980s. Neal Broten played 17 years in the NHL and accumulated more than 900 points. These players helped spark interest in hockey throughout the United States. The number of US hockey players—and US born NHL players—has grown greatly since the 1980 Olympics.

"If anybody in here is surprised we won the gold, let me know," Craig said. "This team put out every game and all I ever tried to do was keep them in it. How many shots did guys block with their heads and their bodies today?"

The celebration that had been ongoing since the United States beat the Soviets continued. Vice President Walter Mondale congratulated the team personally. President Jimmy Carter phoned them to do the same.

For at least one moment, Americans could forget about the troubles of the world and the problems in their lives. They indeed believed in miracles. What that US team achieved was not the first upset in hockey history, though. And it would not be the last. Hockey teams have been shocking fans since the invention of the sport.

THE GOAL THAT UNITED A NATION

Another famous Olympic hockey moment involved Team USA. This time, however, it was not so memorable for the US fans. The 2010 Olympic Winter Games were in Vancouver, Canada—a country that loves its hockey. When Canada met Team USA in the gold-medal game, Canadians saw an opportunity for a gold medal and for bragging rights over their southern neighbors. Canada led near the end of the game. But with only 24 seconds left, Team USA tied the score. Just when Canada needed a hero, the country's biggest hockey star stepped up. Sidney Crosby scored the game-winning goal 7:40 into overtime. It became known as "the goal that united a nation."

Team USA secured the 1980 Olympic gold medal after defeating Finland in its final game.

THE EARLY DAYS

The concept of hockey has been around for thousands of years. Games involving people moving an object with a stick have been traced back to ancient times. People in distant areas such as Scotland, Egypt, and South America all independently played these games. An Irish version of the game was called "Hockie." That is most likely where the modern name of hockey came from.

These games, however, were all played on fields. People in England began standardizing the rules for this game during the 1800s. The result was the sport today known as field hockey.

Canadians were the first to play hockey games on ice. There are different theories as to how the sport originated. Some people

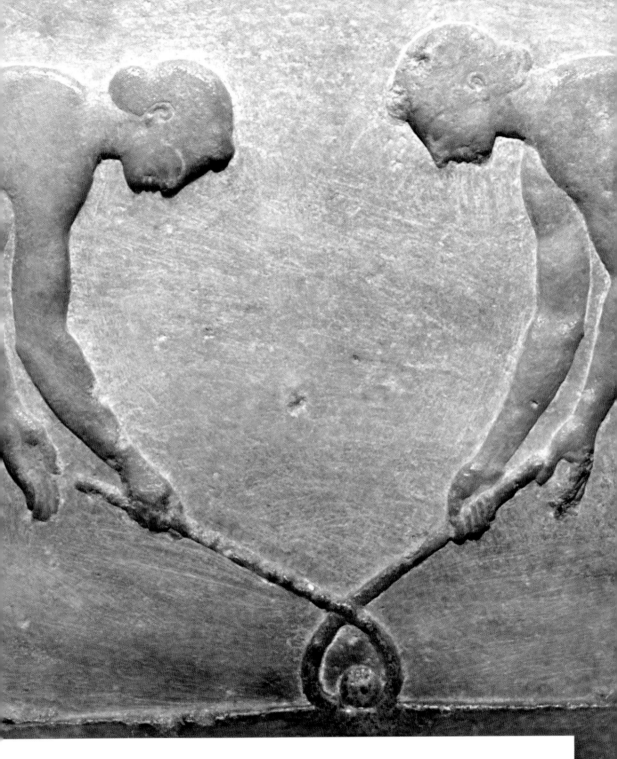

A form of field hockey was being played in the Mediterranean circa 490 BCE.

believe ice hockey was based mostly on English field hockey. However, American Indians in Nova Scotia, Canada, were playing a game similar to ice hockey in the early 1800s. Their game was similar to an Irish version of field hockey. Elements of both English field hockey and the American Indians' game were adopted into ice hockey.

A Canadian named J. G. Creighton is credited with organizing the first ice hockey game and the first set of standardized ice hockey rules in 1875. Two teams from McGill University in Montreal, Canada, played in the first game. That game was very violent. However, it soon began spreading in popularity throughout Canada.

Ice hockey was being played in the United States by 1893. The sport had spread to European countries such as England, Scotland, and France by 1897. And by 1905, organized competition began between squads from France and Belgium.

Soon the sport was in need of an international organization. So in 1908 the International Ice Hockey Federation (IIHF) formed in Paris, France. It began with just five European members. However, the IIHF has grown to become the international governing body for all of ice hockey.

Ice hockey firmly established itself as an international sport in 1920. That year, the sport was contested in the Olympic Games. The Olympics split into a Summer Games and a Winter Games beginning in 1924. Men's ice hockey has been a popular sport in the Olympic Winter Games ever since.

Professional Hockey

Although the IIHF began in Europe, Canadians embraced ice hockey more than any other country. The IIHF even adopted the Canadian rules of hockey first implemented by Creighton.

Amateur hockey leagues formed in Canada and the United States around the turn of the century. Professional leagues soon followed. One was the National Hockey Association (NHA). However, the NHA folded in 1917 when many of its players left to fight in World War I. That was when Toronto Arenas team owner Eddie Livingstone formed the NHL.

The original NHL boasted four Canadian teams. Two were from Montreal, while Ottawa and Toronto each had one team. The Toronto Arenas won the first NHL title in 1918.

The NHL boasted only Canadian teams until 1924. That is when the Boston Bruins became the first team from the United States to join the league. Other US and Canadian teams were

The Montreal Amateur Athletic Association won the first Stanley Cup in 1893. The best Canadian amateur team won the Cup through 1910.

created and then folded over the next 11 years. But the New York Rangers, the Detroit Red Wings, and the Chicago Blackhawks survived. They joined Boston, the Toronto Maple Leafs, and the Montreal Canadiens to form what is known as the "Original Six."

Those six teams battled each other from 1943 until the major NHL expansion in 1967. Though only two teams remained in Canada, they largely dominated the league for more than 30 years. Together, the Maple Leafs and the Canadiens combined to win 19 of the 24 championships from 1944 to 1967.

Lord Stanley's Cup

The Stanley Cup is awarded to the champion of the NHL playoffs. Many consider it to be the most revered trophy in North American professional sports. That is partially because it also happens to be the oldest trophy in North American professional sports.

In 1893, Canadian Governor-General Lord Stanley purchased the trophy for $50. His intention at the time was to present it to the best amateur hockey club in the nation. As such, the earliest winners of the Stanley Cup were amateur teams from Canada.

In 1910, however, professional teams began competing for the cup, including those from the NHA. Since 1927, the Stanley Cup has been awarded to the NHL champion. It has been awarded every year except 2005, when the NHL season was cancelled due to a labor dispute.

AN OCTOPUS FOR GOOD LUCK

In 1952, the Detroit Red Wings had swept the Toronto Maple Leafs in the Stanley Cup semifinals. They then beat the Montreal Canadiens in the first three games of the Stanley Cup Finals. So before Game 4, two Red Wings fans came up with a plan for good luck. Brothers Pete and Jerry Cusimano tossed a small, dead octopus onto the ice. Each of its eight tentacles represented a playoff victory—and the Wings already had seven.

The octopus landed next to referee Frank Udvari. "[Udvari's] face turned white and he backed away from it like it was a hand grenade," Pete Cusimano recalled. But the Red Wings won the game— and the Stanley Cup. The Cusimanos continued throwing an octopus onto the ice during the playoffs for years. Red Wings fans continue this tradition today.

Lord Stanley's Cup is not revered simply for its age, though. The Cup is also famous because the name of every player on the winning squad is inscribed onto the trophy. As more and more players add their names to the Cup each year, the trophy itself has changed. To make room for the names, new bands have been added—and subtracted—under the bowl. Old bands, as well as the original bowl, are on display at the Hockey Hall of Fame in Toronto.

The Women's Game

The first reports of women playing ice hockey came around 1890 in Canada. Like many sports

The original Stanley Cup is on display in the Hockey Hall of Fame in Toronto, Canada.

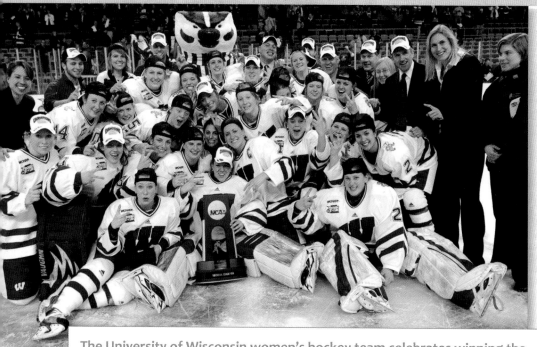

The University of Wisconsin women's hockey team celebrates winning the 2011 NCAA Division I championship.

during that time, the men's game grew much faster than the women's game. That was in part because many people thought it was improper for women to compete in sports—especially grueling sports.

Nevertheless, women's hockey slowly but surely grew. By 1900, three teams formed the first-ever women's hockey league in Quebec, Canada. Women's hockey spread across the US border around that time as well.

Some US colleges began offering women's hockey programs over the next several decades. Providence College, the University of New Hampshire, and Northeastern University offered the first intercollegiate league for women. But opportunities like that were rare. It was not until 1972 that women's hockey truly began to grow. That is when the US government passed Title IX. It said, among other things, that schools had to give equal opportunities for men's and women's sports. After that, more schools and colleges began offering varsity girls' and women's hockey teams.

In 2011, there were more than 50 Division I and III National Collegiate Athletic Association (NCAA) colleges supporting women's teams. There is no Division II in women's hockey. The 2011 numbers were a significant improvement from the emergence of women's college hockey in the 1970s. However, there still remained many more opportunities for boys' and men's hockey players.

DYNASTIES AND DYNAMITE PLAYERS

I t was 1944. The Montreal Canadiens and the Toronto Maple Leafs were battling in the Stanley Cup semifinals. And young Canadiens right wing Maurice "The Rocket" Richard was about to become a star. Montreal coach Dick Irvin had already predicted greatness for Richard. "Not only will he be a star," Irvin had said early that season, "but he'll be the biggest star in hockey."

Irvin was right. And Richard began to prove it against the Maple Leafs. The Canadiens had dominated the NHL all year with an incredible 38–5–7 record. But that would mean nothing if they did not win the Stanley Cup.

So Richard made sure they did. He led the Canadiens to a four-game sweep of the Toronto Maple Leafs in the playoffs'

Maurice "The Rocket" Richard of the Montreal Canadiens was the first NHL player to score 50 goals in 50 games.

first round. He scored all five goals in a Game 2 victory. He then led the team to a four-games-to-one win over the Chicago Blackhawks in the Stanley Cup Finals. Richard set a playoff record by scoring 12 goals in the playoffs that year.

And Richard was just warming up. He became the first player to reach another NHL milestone by scoring 50 goals in 50 games the following year. During one nine-game blitz, he tallied 15 goals, including five in one game. However, the Maple Leafs stunned the Canadiens in the first round of the playoffs that year and later won the championship.

Richard boasted blazing speed on the ice. He was among the top 10 scorers in the NHL every year but two from 1945 through 1957. But it was his passion for the sport that earned him the greatest respect.

WHAT A PERFORMANCE!

Perhaps the most inspiring Stanley Cup performance ever occurred in Game 2 of the 1928 Finals. And it was turned in by a coach. New York Rangers goaltender Lorne Chabot was removed on a stretcher unconscious after being struck in the eye by a puck. Coach Lester Patrick had no replacement, so he took over in goal himself. Patrick was 44 years old. He was a former player, but never a goaltender. Yet Patrick stopped shot after shot. He surrendered just one goal in two periods and overtime. Patrick was given a standing ovation after the Rangers clinched the victory.

Gordie Howe, *center*, retired in 1980 as the NHL's career leader in goals, assists, and points. His first NHL season was 1946–47.

"The Rocket was more than a hockey player," Irvin said. "It was his fury, his desire, and his intensity that motivated the Canadiens."

Gordie The Great

The Canadian domination of the NHL was briefly interrupted by Detroit during the early 1950s. The Red Wings boasted the league's most explosive offensive team through 2011. Detroit's Ted Lindsay and Sid Abel both earned induction into the Hockey Hall of Fame. But right wing Gordie Howe would be recognized as one of the greatest players in league history.

THE FROZEN FOUR

At the end of each college hockey season, 16 men's teams and eight women's teams qualify for the NCAA tournament. The semifinals and finals of those tournaments are known as the Frozen Four.

The NCAA champions often come from areas of the country where ice hockey is popular, such as the Upper Midwest and Northeast. In fact, through 2011, six schools from those areas have won 38 of the 63 men's titles since the event was launched in 1948. Teams from those areas have won every women's title since the women's tournament began in 2001.

On the men's side, the University of Michigan has won the most titles through 2011 with nine. The University of Denver and the University of North Dakota are tied for second with seven titles each. And Boston College and Boston University have combined for nine Frozen Four championships. On the women's side, the University of Minnesota-Duluth leads the way with five titles. The University of Wisconsin is a close second with four titles, and the University of Minnesota has two.

Along with standout goaltender Terry Sawchuk, that trio led Detroit to four Stanley Cup titles. The Red Wings owned the best record in the NHL every year from 1949 to 1955. They won the Stanley Cup in 1950, 1952, 1954, and 1955. And Detroit scored the most goals in the league in all but one of those seasons. Howe led the NHL in points in four straight years.

Howe earned a reputation for his strength, his hard and accurate shot, and his ability to win control of the puck. But he became even better known for his longevity. He played an amazing 32 years in the NHL and the rival World Hockey Association (WHA). He scored more than 100 points at the age of 41, and he did not retire until he

Jacques Plante was the first NHL goalie to wear a mask while playing. Through 2011, he ranked sixth in career wins and fifth in career shutouts.

was 51. It remained the longest playing career in the history of major North American sports through 2011. But even the great Howe could not stop the oncoming era of Canadian dominance.

The New Generation

The Canadiens and the Maple Leafs won 13 of 14 titles from 1956 to 1969. Montreal grabbed the title torch from Detroit and won five straight Stanley Cup crowns in the late 1950s. But it was not Richard or any other scorer that led the way. It was brilliant defenseman Doug Harvey along with Jacques Plante. Many consider Plante to be the greatest goaltender ever.

Bobby Hull led the NHL in goals scored for seven seasons, but his Chicago Blackhawks only managed one Stanley Cup win in three appearances.

Plante gave up an average of 1.86 to 2.54 goals per game every season from 1956 to 1960. He led the NHL in that category all five years. And it was no coincidence that the Canadiens captured Stanley Cup championships in each of those seasons.

By the early 1960s, the Maple Leafs had taken over as the premier team in hockey. But soon, a Blackhawks duo blossomed into the most feared combination in the league. Left wing Bobby Hull and right wing Stan Mikita both finished in the top 10 in scoring every season from 1962 to 1969. They placed first and second three times during one remarkable four-year stretch.

SLAPPING TO SUCCESS

Blackhawks star Bobby Hull did not invent the slap shot. But he certainly shot it with great force. He claimed his slap shot could "take out the backs of chairs at Chicago Stadium." A slap shot is characterized by the backswing to shoulder height. It is the most powerful way of shooting.

Hull gained greater fame and popularity than Mikita. But some believe they were equally talented and that Mikita should have received more recognition.

"[Mikita] is one of the best all-around hockey players I've seen in my life," said Toronto general manager Jim Gregory. "It is just his misfortune that two superstars on the same team cannot share the popularity equally. One is always the darling of the fans while the other works hard for the slightest applause."

More superstars were on their way in the NHL. So was an expansion that would place franchises from coast to coast. In 1967, the league doubled in size. The "Original Six" were sent to the East Division. And the new St. Louis Blues, Philadelphia Flyers, Los Angeles Kings, Pittsburgh Penguins, Minnesota North Stars, and Oakland Seals formed the West Division. A new era in hockey was about to begin.

CHAMPIONS HOME AND ABROAD

M en's ice hockey has been in the Olympic Winter Games since 1920. The IIHF also began holding a separate World Championship event every year beginning in 1930. Canada dominated both competitions during the early years, winning its sixth Olympic gold medal in 1952. The only time Canada failed to win gold was in 1936, when it won silver. Canada had also won nine of the 12 World Championships during that period. But the country's dominance would soon be tested.

In 1954, the Soviet Union's hockey team began competing internationally. It immediately made an impact. The Soviets won the IIHF World Championship that year and the gold medal in the 1956 Winter Games. The Soviet team would go on to dominate international ice hockey for years to come.

The Soviet hockey team poses after defeating Canada for the gold medal at the 1964 Olympic Games.

The First Miracle

In 1960, however, neither the Canadians nor the Soviets left the Olympic Winter Games with the gold medal. The Games that year were held in Squaw Valley, California. Like in 1980, few people figured the US team would have much of a chance against the powerful Soviets and Canadians. But Team USA upset both hockey powers. Center Bill Christian and goaltender Jack McCartan led the way. McCartan made 38 saves in the 2–1 win over Canada. Two days later, Christian scored two goals in the 3–2 defeat of the Soviet Union.

The 1980 US team received great attention for its gold medal. However, the 1960 team received little fame for its victory. That was just fine with US player Bill Cleary, who scored the first goal against Canada.

"I wouldn't trade any chance to march in the Olympics parade of athletes for 100 Stanley Cup

COMPETITION FOR THE NHL

The only major threat for the NHL during its existence came from the WHA. The WHA operated from 1972 to 1979. It made a splash before its first season by signing top NHL players. Bobby Hull left the Chicago Blackhawks to play for the Winnipeg Jets. Toronto Maple Leafs goaltender Bernie Parent defected to the Philadelphia Blazers, but quickly returned to the NHL. And Gordie Howe later played alongside sons Mark and Marty with the WHA Houston Aeros and New England Whalers. The Whalers, the Jets, the Quebec Nordiques, and the Edmonton Oilers all moved to the NHL when the WHA folded in 1979.

championships," he said. "When it was over, we all went back to our lives. That's the way we wanted it."

Neither the US nor Canada would make a habit of winning international competitions, though. The Soviets began a string of nine straight IIHF World Championship gold medals in 1963. And they captured all four Olympic titles from 1964 to 1976. After falling to Team USA in 1980, the Soviet Union went undefeated through the 1984 Games and won Olympic gold in 1988 as well.

The tide had turned in international hockey. And in 1980, it was also beginning to turn in the NHL. Two players in particular brought major changes to the sport.

First Orr, then Gretzky

Until the late 1960s, defensemen took the name of their position literally. They generally just played defense. Then Bobby Orr skated into the league and everything changed.

Orr played brilliant defense for the Boston Bruins. But Orr also emerged as one of the most prolific scorers in the NHL. He scored at least 100 points in every season from 1970 to 1975. He also led the league in points in 1970 and 1975. And he was number one in assists five times.

Bobby Orr still held the NHL record for points in a season by a defenseman in 2011. He scored 139 points during the 1970–71 season.

The Bruins had not won a Stanley Cup title for 29 years until Orr came along. But with Orr leading the charge, they won it in both 1970 and 1972. After scoring the game-winning goal to secure the 1970 Stanley Cup, Orr was tripped. A photo of him flying through the air, parallel to the ice with his arms out in celebration became one of the most famous images in sports.

Orr played a position in which players were not known for scoring. Wayne Gretzky, on the other hand, played center, where players are often expected to score. But Gretzky scored more than any NHL player ever. And when he retired in 1999, most considered him the greatest player who ever lived. In fact, many people refer to him simply as "The Great One."

Gretzky shattered every league scoring record. In 1982, he became the first player to tally 200 points in a season. He led the NHL in scoring 11 years, including eight in a row from 1980 to 1987. Gretzky paced the league in assists in 13 straight seasons. And when he finally hung up his skates, he had scored 2,857 points. That is nearly 1,000 more than any other player in league history.

After nine dominant seasons with the Edmonton Oilers, Gretzky was sent to the Los Angeles Kings in a blockbuster trade. His popularity helped grow hockey in the United States' second largest city. He even led the Kings to the Stanley Cup Finals in 1993. But midway through his eighth season in Los Angeles,

Gretzky was traded to the St. Louis Blues. He spent his final three seasons with the New York Rangers. Even though Gretzky played much of his NHL career in the United States, he remains a national hero in Canada.

Author and sports analyst John Feinstein was one of millions of hockey fans who marveled at Gretzky.

"I think the best description I ever heard of him came from other players who said that when Wayne was on the ice, you thought he had eyes not just in the front of his head but on the sides and back of his head," Feinstein said. "The statistic that you come back to among all those records is that he had more assists—setting up other players to score—in his career than any other player in history has goals and assists combined."

THE BROAD STREET BULLIES

Perhaps the roughest, toughest NHL champions of all-time were the mid-1970s Philadelphia Flyers. They were so rugged that they were known as the "Broad Street Bullies." They scrapped their way to Stanley Cup championships in 1974 and 1975. The Flyers were led offensively by center Bobby Clarke and forward Rick MacLeish, as well as goaltender Bernie Parent. But the biggest "bully" of all was left wing Dave "The Hammer" Schultz, who spent much of his playing time fighting on the ice. The 1974 Flyers led the NHL with an incredible 1,750 penalty minutes.

The New Dynasties

The Montreal Canadiens had more than five NHL opponents

Wayne Gretzky was still the NHL's all-time leader in points, assists, and goals through 2011.

to beat by the late-1970s. Yet they still won four straight Stanley Cup titles from 1976 to 1979. The NHL had 17 teams by the end of that decade. But that is when the Canadiens' run of dominance ended. And in the 1980s, two teams that had existed for fewer than 10 years forged dynasties of their own.

"MIRACLE ON MANCHESTER"

The NHL playoffs have featured many upsets over the years. But none stunned the hockey world more than the Los Angeles Kings' upset of the powerful Edmonton Oilers in 1982. The Kings finished the regular season 48 points behind the Oilers in the standings. The teams split the first two games in their series. Then the Oilers took a 5–0 lead in Game 3. The Kings rallied back to make the score 5–4. As the final seconds ticked away, it seemed certain their comeback had fallen short. But with five seconds remaining, Kings player Steve Bozek scored to tie the game. And less than three minutes into overtime, Kings rookie Daryl Evans smacked the puck into the net to win it. The Kings eventually won the series. The shocking upset is known as "The Miracle on Manchester" because the Kings' home arena rested on Manchester Boulevard.

"We were just a group of guys, mostly on the young side, who believed in ourselves," Evans said.

The first was the New York Islanders. The Islanders won with a smothering defense and a high-scoring right wing named Mike Bossy. They captured four consecutive Stanley Cup championships from 1980 to 1983. And they played their best with the title on the line. The Islanders won 16 of 19 games in Stanley Cup Finals during that stretch. They embarked on four-game sweeps in both 1982 and 1983.

But when Gretzky got on a roll, no team could stop his Oilers. Edmonton snagged four of five NHL crowns from 1984 to 1988. And Gretzky received plenty of help from high-scoring forward Mark Messier and top goaltender Grant Fuhr.

Mike Bossy celebrates his goal in Game 4 of the Stanley Cup Finals against the Vancouver Canucks in 1982. Bossy's New York Islanders swept the series.

No NHL team would again be as dominant as the Islanders and the Oilers had been in the 1980s. But a sensational player in Pittsburgh would soon remind fans of Gretzky. And another Midwest team would later emerge as the best heading into the new millennium and beyond.

CHAPTER 5

THE SHRINKING WORLD OF HOCKEY

Few raised an eyebrow in 1973 when Swedish defenseman Borje Salming blossomed with the Toronto Maple Leafs. He was the first European-trained player to become an NHL star. But changes in the world had brought changes to hockey. In the early 1980s, the relationship between the Soviet Union and the United States remained strained. That made it impossible for Eastern Bloc players to compete in the NHL.

The Montreal Canadiens drafted legendary Soviet goaltender Vladislav Tretiak in 1983. However, he was not allowed to join the team. There was still one way Eastern Bloc players could join the NHL. Brothers Peter and Anton Stastny defected from Czechoslovakia and joined the Quebec Nordiques in 1980. Their oldest brother Marian Stastny joined them the next season.

The Washington Capitals' Alex Ovechkin, *front*, and the Pittsburgh Penguins' Evgeni Malkin, *back*, are both Russians who have found success in the NHL.

All three became top NHL players. But Peter Stastny was the best. Only Wayne Gretzky had more points than Peter during the 1980s.

More Eastern Bloc players began defecting after the Stastny brothers. Still, the Soviets remained an international hockey power. They won their seventh Olympic gold medal in 1988. But the Communist government in that country was beginning to collapse. As such, the Soviets' hold on other Eastern European countries was weakening. Soon, players from those countries were free to join the NHL.

Players from countries such as Czechoslovakia entered the NHL. But the Russians poured into the league. Russia was the largest country to emerge out of the Soviet Union when it fell in 1991. By 2001, 58 Russian players were playing in the NHL. And many of the league's premier players in the 1990s and 2000s were Russian. Included was center and six-time All-Star Sergei Fedorov.

Perhaps the best of all Russian players, though, was Washington Capitals left wing Alex Ovechkin. He led the NHL in goals and points in 2008. Ovechkin blossomed into a back-to-back Most Valuable Player (MVP) in 2007–08 and 2008–09.

CUP FOR A DAY

It is an NHL tradition that every player and employee from the Stanley Cup-winning team gets to keep the Cup for one day. This has led to some mischief. In 1905, a member of the Ottawa Senators kicked the Cup into a canal. It was not fished out until the next day. Two years later, the Montreal Wanderers gave it to a photographer. His mother used it as a flowerpot. New York Rangers player Eddie Olczyk let racehorse Go for Gin drink out of the Cup in 1994. And Detroit Red Wings captain Steve Yzerman once took a shower with it in his bathroom.

Women's Growth

While men's hockey thrived on the college, professional, and Olympic levels for much of the twentieth century, organized women's hockey went largely unnoticed. That began to change at the college level with Title IX in 1972. And the legislation actually helped spur the growth of the game at all levels. Women's hockey took another major step forward in 1990. That is when the IIHF held the first World Women's Championship, which was played in Canada.

The women who played in the first World Championship were the original pioneers of the game. Since there were very few girls' leagues, many of those players grew up playing on boys' teams. In the years that followed, girls' hockey leagues became more common across the United States and Canada. The World

Cammi Granato, *left*, and Karyn Bye show off their Olympic gold medals. They led Team USA to the first Olympic women's hockey title in 1998.

Championship event also introduced the first stars of women's hockey with players such as Angela James of Canada and Cindy Curley of the United States.

The World Championship was played four times between 1990 and 1997. Each tournament had a familiar ending: Canada won, the United States took second, and Finland took third. By 1998, the International Olympic Committee deemed women's hockey popular enough around the world to be part of the Olympic Winter Games.

Six teams came to Nagano, Japan, for the 1998 Games. Many favored Canada to continue its dominance by winning the gold medal. But behind star forward Cammi Granato, Team USA was ready to put up a fight. When Canada and the United States met in a first-round game, Canada took a 4–1 lead midway through the third period. But Team USA came back to win 7–4.

As expected, the teams again met in the gold-medal game. And Team USA again defeated Canada. US veteran Shelley Looney scored the game-winning goal in Team USA's 3–1 victory.

That triumph proved historic for women's hockey in the United States. In the years that followed the 1998 Games, the number of girls registered to play hockey in the United States skyrocketed. Meanwhile, on the international level, Canada and the United States continued to dominate. Through 2011, the World Women's

A WOMEN'S STAR

Nobody was more responsible for the growing popularity of women's hockey than Illinois native Cammi Granato. She received a full scholarship in 1989 from Providence College—one of the few schools to recruit women's players at that time. She dominated at the college level, scoring 135 goals and adding 110 assists in just 93 games. But Granato gained her greatest fame in the first Olympic women's hockey competition in 1998. She tallied four goals and four assists in leading Team USA to a gold medal.

"When you think women's hockey, you think Cammi Granato," said Mike Eruzione, captain of the US men's 1980 Olympic championship team. "She's one of the pioneers. So many little girls wanted to be Cammi Granato." In 2010, Granato and Angela James of Canada became the first women to be inducted into the Hockey Hall of Fame.

Championship had been held 13 times. The United States and Canada met in the finals all 13 times. However, after eight silver medals, Team USA finally won the tournament for the first time in 2005. The Americans followed that with three consecutive gold medals at the World Championships, in 2008, 2009, and 2011. There was no World Championship in 2010 because of the 2010 Winter Games.

Other countries have shown improvement in women's hockey. Since 1990, Finland and Sweden have often met in the bronze-medal game at the World Women's Championship and Winter Games. And at the 2006 Olympic Winter Games, Sweden stunned the favored US team with a 3–2 overtime win in the semifinals. That earned the Swedes a berth into the finals, where they won their only silver medal in Olympic women's

THE "BUTTERFLY" STYLE

Goaltenders Patrick Roy and Martin Brodeur are known for using the "butterfly" style. A butterfly style goaltender drops to his or her knees with his or her feet flared to each side when a shot is taken. This allows the goaltender to cover the lower part of the net with their legs and rely on their glove and blocker (hands) to stop shots intended for the upper corners of the net. Brodeur grew up idolizing Roy. He was 14 years old when Roy won a Stanley Cup with the Montreal Canadiens.

hockey. Through 2010, that marked the only time Team USA and Canada did not play each other for the Olympic gold medal.

At the 2010 Winter Games, Canada defeated Team USA on its home ice in Vancouver to win its third straight gold medal. And that final game featured four players who had played against each other at the 1998 gold-medal game. They were forward Jenny Potter and defenseman Angela Ruggiero from Team USA, and forwards Jennifer Botterill and Hayley Wickenheiser from Canada. Those players have helped grow the game and inspire a whole new generation of women's hockey stars in North America.

Expansion from Coast to Coast

The days of dynasties in the NHL were over by 2000. That year, the league expanded to its current 30 teams. And those teams were in cities all across the United States and Canada, from Florida to Southern California, and from Montreal to Vancouver. As of 2011, no NHL team had won more than two straight Stanley Cup championships since 1983. None had even captured two in a row since 1998. And no Canadian team has earned the title since Montreal in 1993.

The Detroit Red Wings were the last team to repeat as NHL champions through 2011. They won the Stanley Cup in 1997 and 1998.

Despite the balance in the league, three teams in the modern era rose above the rest. One was the Detroit Red Wings. They have not suffered through a losing season from 1991 through 2011. The Red Wings won the Stanley Cup title in 1997, 1998, 2002, and 2008.

The offensive talents of Fedorov and center Steve Yzerman played major roles on the first three championship teams. But perhaps no Red Wings player was more responsible for their success than Nicklas Lidstrom. The Swede joined the Red Wings

LIGHTS OUT

Game 4 of the 1988 Stanley Cup Finals started on time. But it did not end on time. The battle between the Edmonton Oilers and the Boston Bruins was tied when it was postponed in the second period. A power failure had made it pitch-black at Boston Garden. The game was moved to Edmonton, where the Oilers finished off their four-game sweep.

in 1991 and was still with the team following the 2010–11 season. He is considered one of the finest defensemen who ever laced up a pair of skates.

The New Jersey Devils were also a powerhouse. They won Stanley Cup titles in 1995, 2000, and 2003. Goaltender Martin Brodeur led those teams. Brodeur, whose 20-year playing career continued in 2011, has led the NHL in victories nine times. He has given up an average of just 2.22 goals per game.

The Pittsburgh Penguins also experienced great success. They won successive titles in 1991 and 1992. The Penguins of that era were led by brilliant center Mario Lemieux. He amazed hockey players, coaches, and fans from the start of his career. "Once he gets behind you, he cannot be legally stopped," one-time Penguins coach Gene Ubriaco said.

Few could have imagined how great Lemieux would become. He picked up where Gretzky left off as the most prolific scorer in the league. He topped the NHL in points six times from 1988 to 1997. However, after the 1996–97 season, he retired at age 31. Lemieux had suffered years of injuries, including a bout with cancer.

In 1999, the Penguins were on the verge of bankruptcy. There was a chance they would have to move to another city. So Lemieux bought the club and vowed to keep it in Pittsburgh. One year later, in 2000–01, he returned to the ice and played five more seasons.

Lemieux's final season ended up being the first season of hockey's next big superstar. In 2005, the Penguins selected Sidney Crosby with the first pick in the NHL draft. The center debuted with the Penguins in 2005–06. Crosby was just 19 years old when he finished his first NHL season with 102 points. He led the league with 120 points the following season.

THE WINTER CLASSIC

The NHL hit on a popular promotion in 2008 when it launched the annual Winter Classic. The regular-season game is played outdoors at baseball or football stadiums on New Year's Day. The event has drawn huge crowds. The first Winter Classic was played in Buffalo before 71,217 fans. Through 2011, every game since has been played to a sellout. Canadian teams have also competed against each other in an outdoor game called the Heritage Classic in 2003 and 2011.

The NHL's Winter Classic brought professional hockey into the elements at outdoor stadiums. The 2009 game was held at Wrigley Field in Chicago.

New Beginnings

The emergence of young stars such as Crosby and Ovechkin came at a time when the NHL needed it most. In 2004–05, the NHL owners and players could not agree on new labor conditions. That resulted in the entire season—including the Stanley Cup playoffs—being cancelled. Through 2011, it was the only time in NHL history that the Stanley Cup was not awarded. Hockey fans became bitter and angry over the loss of their sport. Many people stopped going to games and watching them on TV in the years that followed.

Sidney Crosby became the youngest captain to lead his team to the Stanley Cup title when his Pittsburgh Penguins won in 2009.

With Lemieux and Gretzky retired, the NHL needed new stars to help win back its fans. The league found those stars in Crosby and Ovechkin. The Washington Capitals picked Ovechkin with the first pick in the 2004 draft—one year prior to the Penguins' drafting Crosby. Since the NHL season was cancelled in 2004, Ovechkin played one more season in Russia. And both Ovechkin and Crosby debuted in the NHL in 2005.

Both players starred soon after joining the NHL. Ovechkin won the Calder Trophy in the 2005 as the NHL's Rookie of the Year. He then won back-to-back Hart Trophies (MVP as voted by media) and three straight Ted Lindsay Awards (MVP as voted by players) in 2007–08, 2008–09, and 2009–10. Crosby won the Hart Trophy in 2006–07. But he also won something more important: the Stanley Cup. In 2009, Crosby became the youngest captain to lead his team to the Stanley Cup championship when his Penguins beat the Red Wings in seven games.

Behind young players such as Crosby, Ovechkin, and Tampa Bay Lightning center Steven Stamkos, as well as young women's stars such as Jessie Vetter and Hilary Knight, the future for hockey has never looked brighter.

TIMELINE

1875	Canadian J. G. Creighton creates the first rules for ice hockey.
1877	Creighton coaches McGill University to victory in the first organized ice hockey game on January 31 in Montreal, Canada.
1908	The IIHF is formed in Paris on May 15.
1917	The NHL is born with four Canadian teams.
1920	Ice hockey is accepted as an Olympic sport.
1924	The Boston Bruins are awarded the first US NHL franchise.
1943	The "Original Six" franchises of the Montreal Canadiens, the Toronto Maple Leafs, the New York Rangers, the Boston Bruins, the Detroit Red Wings, and the Chicago Blackhawks are established in the NHL.
1952	Canada wins its sixth Olympic gold medal. But it would be its last for 50 years.
1956	The Soviet Union enters Olympic hockey competition for the first time and takes the gold.
1960	Montreal becomes the first NHL team to win five straight Stanley Cup titles, completing a Finals sweep of Toronto on April 14. The United States wins the Olympic gold medal on February 28, with a 9–4 win over Czechoslovakia.
1967	The NHL doubles its number of teams with its first major expansion.
1972	Title IX is enacted, spurring the growth of women's hockey in the United States.

1978 — Center Wayne Gretzky joins the Edmonton Oilers and embarks on perhaps the greatest offensive career in NHL history.

1980 — The US team stuns the Soviets 4–3 on February 22 in the greatest hockey upset in Olympic history, known as the Miracle on Ice. Team USA captures the gold medal on February 24 with a 4–2 win over Finland.

1983 — The New York Islanders clinch their fourth straight Stanley Cup on May 17 with a 4–2 defeat of the Edmonton Oilers.

1990 — The first IIHF World Women's Championship is played. Host Canada defeats the United States for the title.

1998 — Professional players are given permission to compete in the Olympic Games, leading to Canada and the United States playing for gold medals in 2002 and 2010. The US women's team beats Canada 3–1 to clinch the first Olympic women's hockey gold medal on February 17.

2004 — A labor dispute between players and owners begins and wipes out the NHL season.

2005 — The United States wins its first IIHF World Women's Championship.

2008 — The first Winter Classic is held at Ralph Wilson Stadium in Buffalo, New York. The Buffalo Sabres beat the Pittsburgh Penguins 2–1 in a shootout.

2009 — Sidney Crosby becomes the youngest captain to lead his team to the Stanley Cup title when his Pittsburgh Penguins defeat the Detroit Red Wings.

2010 — Angela James of Canada and Cammi Granato of the United States are the first women inducted into the Hockey Hall of Fame. Canada sweeps the men's and women's Olympic gold medals on home ice at the Winter Games in Vancouver.

LEGENDS OF HOCKEY

MEN

Mike Bossy
Canada, wing

Wayne Gretzky
Canada, center

Ted Lindsay
Canada, wing

Herb Brooks
United States, coach

Doug Harvey
Canada, defenseman

Stan Mikita
Czechoslovakia, center

Bobby Clarke
Canada, center

Gordie Howe
Canada, wing

Bobby Orr
Canada, defenseman

Jim Craig
United States, goaltender

Bobby Hull
Canada, wing

Jacques Plante
Canada, goaltender

Sidney Crosby
Canada, center

Mark Johnson
United States, center

Maurice Richard
Canada, wing

Mike Eruzione
United States, wing

Mario Lemieux
Canada, center

Terry Sawchuk
Canada, goaltender

Sergei Fedorov
Russia, center

Nicklas Lidstrom
Sweden, defenseman

Vladislav Tretiak
Soviet Union, goaltender

WOMEN

Cammi Granato
United States, forward

Shelley Looney
United States, forward

Angela Ruggiero
United States, defenseman

Angela James
Canada, center

Jenny Potter
United States, forward

Hayley Wickenheiser
Canada, forward

GLOSSARY

assist
A pass to a teammate that is turned into a goal.

center
The middle forward in a line who is greatly responsible for offense.

defect
To leave one's country secretly for another.

defensemen
Players on the ice mostly trying to prevent opponents from scoring.

dynasty
A team that wins many championships during a short period of time.

expansion
The adding of franchises to a league.

finals
The final playoff series that determines a league champion.

forward
One of three offensive-minded players consisting of a center and two wings.

goaltender
The player protecting the goal and trying to keep the puck out of the net.

period
A segment of time in a hockey game. Hockey games are divided into three periods.

rink
The ice surface on which hockey games are played.

rivalry
An intense feeling between two teams.

save
The goaltender's stop of a puck that is heading into the net.

Stanley Cup
The annual NHL playoffs, as well as the trophy won by the championship team.

upset
An unexpected victory by one team over another.

wings
Two of three forward positions on a hockey team.

Selected Bibliography

Davidson, Ron. *Play Better Hockey: 50 Essential Skills for Player Development.* Buffalo, NY: Firefly Books, 2010. Print.

McFarlane, Brian. *Legendary Stanley Cup Stories.* Boston, MA: Fenn Publishing Company, 2008. Print.

NHL Public Relations Department. *National Hockey League Official Guide & Record Book 2011.* Chicago: Triumph Books, 2010. Print.

Zweig, Eric, James Duplacey, and Dan Diamond. *The Ultimate Prize: The Stanley Cup.* Kansas City, MO: Andrews McMeel, 2003. Print.

Further Readings

Carroll, Michael. *The Concise Encyclopedia of Hockey.* Toronto: Greystone Books, 2003. Print.

Doeden, Matt. *Wayne Gretzky (Sports Heroes and Legends).* Minneapolis, MN: Twenty-First Century Books, 2007. Print.

McKinley, Michael. *Ice Time: The Story of Hockey.* Toronto: Tundra Books, 2006. Print.

Stout, Glenn and Matt Christopher. *On the Ice with … Mario Lemieux.* New York: Little, Brown Books for Young Readers, 2002. Print.

Web Links

To learn more about hockey, visit ABDO Publishing Company online at **www.abdopublishing.com**. Web sites about hockey are featured on our Book Links page. These links are routinely monitored and updated to provide the most current information available.

Places to Visit

Hockey Hall of Fame

30 Yonge Street
Toronto, ON M5E 1X8, Canada
(416) 360-7735
www.hhof.com

This hall of fame celebrates the history of hockey and its greatest players and contributors through memorabilia and other interactive exhibits. Among the highlights of the museum is the opportunity to view the original Stanley Cup trophy. The Hall is located in downtown Toronto, not far from the Maple Leafs' home arena.

US Hockey Hall of Fame and Museum

801 Hat Trick Avenue
P.O. Box 679
Eveleth, MN 55734
(800) 443-7825
www.ushockeyhall.com

Located in northern Minnesota, this hall of fame and museum celebrates the history of US hockey through various exhibits. It also contains an ice rink.

INDEX

About the Author

Marty Gitlin is a freelance writer based in Cleveland, Ohio. He has written more than 40 educational books. Gitlin has won more than 45 awards during his 25 years as a writer, including first place for general excellence from the Associated Press. He lives with his wife and three children.